SECOND EDITION

English Across the Curriculum

Content-area Vocabulary and Skills

1

Margaret Martin Maggs

National Textbook Company
a division of NTC/CONTEMPORARY PUBLISHING COMPANY
Lincolnwood, Illinois USA

ISBN: 0-8442-0289-4

Contents

1A Classroom Directions 1
    1B Classroom Directions 3

2A Subject Names 5
    2B Subject Names 7

3A Social Studies Vocabulary 9
    3B Social Studies Vocabulary 11

4A Math Vocabulary 13
    4B Math Vocabulary 15

5A Science Vocabulary 17
    5B Science Vocabulary 19

6A English Vocabulary 21
    6B English Vocabulary 23

7A Computer Vocabulary 25
    7B Computer Vocabulary 27

8A Art Vocabulary 29
    8B Music Vocabulary 31

9A Social Studies—Maps 33
    9B Social Studies—Maps 35

10A Mathematics—Functions 37
    10B Mathematics—Functions 39

11A Science Vocabulary—Earth 41
    11B Science Vocabulary—Weather 43

12A English Vocabulary—Punctuation 45
    12B English Vocabulary—Punctuation 47

13A Social Studies—States 49
    13B Social Studies—States 51

14A Math Word Problems 53
    14B Math Word Problems 55

15A More Math Word Problems 57
    15B More Math Word Problems 59

Classroom Directions

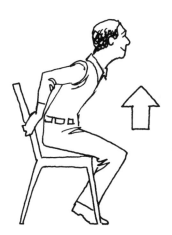

Stand up.

Sit down.

Answer the question.

Raise your hand.

Please be quiet.

Copy the work.

Stand up.
Sit down.
Answer the question.
Raise your hand.
Please be quiet.
Copy the work.

What do you do in school?

_____ a) Stand up.

_____ b) Sit down.

✔ c) Please be quiet.

1. _____ a) Please be quiet.

_____ b) Answer the question.

_____ c) Raise your hand.

4. _____ a) Please be quiet.

_____ b) Answer the question.

_____ c) Raise your hand.

2. _____ a) Stand up.

_____ b) Sit down.

_____ c) Please be quiet.

5. _____ a) Stand up.

_____ b) Sit down.

_____ c) Please be quiet.

3. _____ a) Copy the work.

_____ b) Answer the question.

_____ c) Please be quiet.

6. _____ a) Copy the work.

_____ b) Answer the question.

_____ c) Please be quiet.

ASK A FRIEND

Stand up.   Please be quiet.
Sit down.   Raise your hand.

Read.

Write.

Open your book.

Close your book.

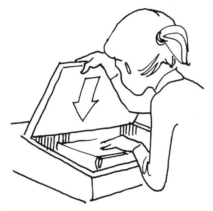

Put away your book.

Take out your book.

Read.
Write.
Open your book.
Close your book.
Put away your book.
Take out your book.

What do you do in school?

EXAMPLE: _____ a) Read.

      ✔ b) Write.

     _____ c) Put away your book.

1. _____ a) Close your book.

  _____ b) Put away your book.

  _____ c) Take out your book.

2. _____ a) Write.

  _____ b) Open your book.

  _____ c) Read.

3. _____ a) Read.

  _____ b) Open your book.

  _____ c) Write.

4. _____ a) Close your book.

  _____ b) Take out your book.

  _____ c) Open your book.

5. _____ a) Read.

  _____ b) Put away your book.

  _____ c) Take out your book.

6. _____ a) Write.

  _____ b) Open your book.

  _____ c) Put away your book.

ASK A FRIEND

Take out your book. Close your book.
Open your book.   Read.
Write.   Put away your book.

Subject Names

What are your subjects?

You are a student. You go to school. The subjects you study are:

English   Social Studies   Math   Science

You study <u>Social Studies</u>.

You study <u>English</u>.

You study <u>Science</u>.

You study <u>Math</u> (Mathematics).

5

What are your subjects?

EXAMPLE: Do you study German?   Yes _____   No __✔__

1. Do you study Science?   Yes _____   No _____

2. Do you study English?   Yes _____   No _____

3. Do you study Math?   Yes _____   No _____

4. Do you study Social Studies?   Yes _____   No _____

What subjects do you have?

	English	Math	Science	Social Studies

5. I have _____

6. I have _____

7. I have _____

8. I have _____

ASK A FRIEND

Do you study English?   Do you study Science?
Do you study Math?   Do you study Social Studies?

What are your subjects?

You are a student. You go to school. You take subjects. Sometimes they are:
Art   Music   Computer   Gym

You take <u>Music</u>.

You take <u>Art</u>.

You take <u>Computer</u>.

Almost eight million people live in New York City. More people live in this city than in any other city in the United States■

You take <u>Gym</u>.

Subjects

I study many subjects. They are English, Social Studies, Science and Math. Sometimes I have Art, Music, Gym and Computer.

What are your subjects in the afternoon?

EXAMPLE: Do you have Shop?   Yes _____   No _✔_

1. Do you have Music?   Yes _____   No _____

2. Do you have Gym?   Yes _____   No _____

Almost eight million people live in New York City. More people live in this city than in any other city in the United States■

3. Do you have Computer? Yes _____   No _____

4. Do you have Art?   Yes _____   No _____

What subjects do you take?

	Computer	Gym	Art	Music

5. I take _____

6. I take _____

7. I take _____

8. I take _____

ASK A FRIEND

Do you have Gym?   Do you have Computer?
Do you have Music?   Do you have Art?

Social Studies Vocabulary

What words do you know in Social Studies?

I take Social Studies. I'm learning new
words in Social Studies. They are:

book   map   world   country   nation

This is my Social Studies <u>book</u>.

It has a <u>map</u>.

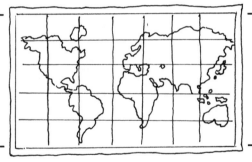

This is a map of the <u>world</u>.

This is a <u>country</u>.
A country is a <u>nation</u>.

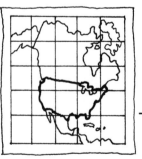

Social Studies

   In Social Studies we study about many nations. The Social
Studies book has maps. It has a big map of the world. It has
maps of countries, too.

What words do you know in Social Studies?

This is my Social Studies _____*book*_____ .
map   world   book

What is this?
It's a ____*book*____ .

1. This is a _____ .
   world   book   country

2. This book has a _____ .
   world   book   map

3. This is a map of the _____ .
   country   world   nation

4. A country is a _____ .
   nation   map   world

5. What is this?

   It's a _____ .

6. What's this?

   It's a _____ .

7. What's this?

   It's a map of the _____ .

8. What's a country?

   It's a _____ .

ASK A FRIEND

Please open your Social Studies book.
Please show me a map.
Please show me a map of the world.

Please show me a map of a country.
What is the name of that nation?

10

What words do you know in Social Studies?

Here are more new words in Social Studies:
city people ocean river land

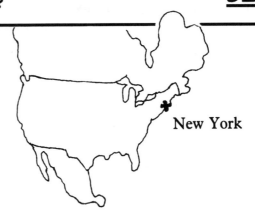

New York

This is a <u>city</u>. Chicago, Los Angeles, Houston and Miami are cities, too. Many <u>people</u> live in a city.

On this map there is an <u>ocean</u>. It is the Atlantic Ocean.

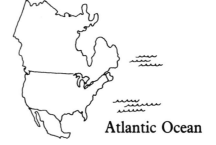

Atlantic Ocean

On this map there is a <u>river</u>. It is the Mississippi River.

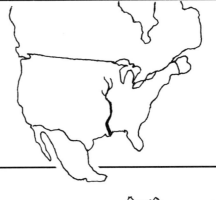

On this map there are two oceans, and there is <u>land</u>. The land is the United States of America, Canada and Mexico.

Social Studies

In the Social Studies book there is a map. It is a map of North America. On the map there are oceans, rivers, cities and countries. One country is the United States. Many people live in the United States.

What words do you know in Social Studies?

EXAMPLES:

There are oceans, and there is _____ *land* _____.
river   city   land

What is this?

This is _____ *land* _____.
city   people   land

1. In a city there are many _____.
   river   land   people

2. This is a _____.
   river   city   people

3. On this map there is an _____.
   ocean   city   people

4. On the map there is a _____.
   city   river   people

5. What's this?

   This is a _____.
   city   people   river

6. What are these?

   These are _____.
   people   city   land

7. What's this?

   It's an _____.
   city   people   ocean

8. What's this?

   It's a _____.
   people   city   river

ASK A FRIEND

Please open your Social Studies book and show me a map of the world.
Please show me the oceans.
Please show me the land.
Please show me a city on the map.

Math Vocabulary

What words do you know in Math?

I take Math. I'm learning new words in Math. They are:

number   add   subtract   multiply   divide

These are <u>numbers</u>.

$$1, 2, 3, 4, 5, 6, 7, 8, 9, 10$$

We <u>add</u> numbers in Math.

$$341 + 802 = 1,143$$

$$\begin{array}{r} 65 \\ +42 \\ \hline 107 \end{array}$$

We <u>subtract</u> numbers in Math.

$$444 - 123 = 321$$

$$\begin{array}{r} 77 \\ -16 \\ \hline 61 \end{array}$$

We <u>multiply</u> numbers in Math.

$$22 \times 2 = 44 \quad 5 \times 5 = 25$$

$$5 \cdot 5 = 25$$

We <u>divide</u> numbers in Math.

$$2 \div 2 = 1 \quad 10 \div 2 = 5$$

$$2 \overline{)100} \quad = 50$$

Math

In Math we study numbers. We add numbers. We subtract numbers. We multiply numbers, and we divide them.

What words do you know in Math?

EXAMPLES:

We _____*subtract*_____ numbers.
add   subtract   numbers

$$\begin{array}{r} 77 \\ -16 \\ \hline 61 \end{array}$$

What do we do in math?

We _____*divide*_____ numbers.

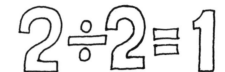

$$1, 2, 3, 4, 5, 6, 7, 8, 9, 10$$

1. We study _____.
   numbers   add   multiply

$$22 \times 2 = 44 \qquad 5 \cdot 5 = 25$$

2. We _____ numbers.
   add   multiply   divide

$$10 \div 2 = 5 \qquad 2\overline{)100}^{\,50}$$

3. We _____ numbers.
   multiply   subtract   divide

$$341 + 802 = 1,143 \qquad \begin{array}{r} 65 \\ +42 \\ \hline 107 \end{array}$$

4. We _____ numbers.
   add   subtract   numbers

$$5 \times 5 = 25$$

5. What do we do in Math?

   We _____ numbers.

$$444 - 123 = 321$$

6. What do we do in Math?

   We _____ numbers.

$$\begin{array}{r} 65 \\ +42 \\ \hline 107 \end{array}$$

7. What do we do in Math?

   We _____ numbers.

$$1, 2, 3, 4, 5, 6, 7, 8, 9, 10$$

8. What are these?

   They're _____.

ASK A FRIEND

Please write two numbers.
Please add the numbers.
Please subtract one number from the other.

Please multiply the numbers.
Please divide one number by the other.

What words do you know in Math?

Here are more new words in Math. They are:

problem addition subtraction
multiplication division

In Math we do <u>problems</u>.	$2+2=4$ $\begin{array}{r}2\\+2\\\hline4\end{array}$ $\begin{array}{r}2\\-2\\\hline0\end{array}$ $\begin{array}{r}2\\\times2\\\hline4\end{array}$ $2\div2=1$ $2-2=0$ $2\cdot2=4$ $2\times2=4$ $2\div2=1$ $2\overline{)2}$
We do <u>addition</u> problems.	$341+802=1{,}143$ $\begin{array}{r}65\\+42\\\hline107\end{array}$
We do <u>subtraction</u> problems.	$444-123=321$ $\begin{array}{r}77\\-16\\\hline61\end{array}$
We do <u>multiplication</u> problems.	$22\times2=44$ $5\times5=25$ $5\cdot5=25$
We do <u>division</u> problems.	$2\div2=1$ $10\div2=5$ $2\overline{)100}\;50$

Math

In Math we have number problems. We add in the addition problems. We subtract in the subtraction problems. We multiply in the multiplication problems. We divide in the division problems.

What words do you know in Math?

EXAMPLES:

$5 \times 5 = 25$

We do ___*multiplication*___ problems.
addition   multiplication   subtraction

$5 \cdot 5 = 25$

What are these problems?

$341 + 802 = 1{,}143$

$$\begin{array}{r} 65 \\ +42 \\ \hline 107 \end{array}$$

They are ___*addition*___ problems.

$341 + 802 = 1{,}143$

$$\begin{array}{r} 2 \\ +2 \\ \hline 4 \end{array} \quad \begin{array}{r} 2 \\ -2 \\ \hline 0 \end{array} \quad \begin{array}{r} 2 \\ \times 2 \\ \hline 4 \end{array} \quad \begin{array}{l} 2 \div 2 = 1 \\ 2 \cdot 2 = 4 \end{array} \quad 2\overline{)2}$$

1. We do _____ problems.
   subtraction   problems   addition

3. We do number _____.
   problems   division   addition

$444 - 123 = 321$

$$\begin{array}{r} 77 \\ -16 \\ \hline 61 \end{array}$$

$2 \div 2 = 1$

$$2\overline{)100}\ \ ^{50}$$

2. We do _____ problems.
   addition   subtraction   division

4. We do _____ problems.
   division   multiplication   problems

$2 \div 2 = 1$

$$2\overline{)100}\ \ ^{50}$$

5. What are these?

   They're _____ problems.

$444 - 123 = 321$

$$\begin{array}{r} 77 \\ -16 \\ \hline 61 \end{array}$$

7. What are these?

   They're _____ problems.

$$\begin{array}{r} 2 \\ +2 \\ \hline 4 \end{array} \quad \begin{array}{r} 2 \\ -2 \\ \hline 0 \end{array} \quad \begin{array}{r} 2 \\ \times 2 \\ \hline 4 \end{array} \quad \begin{array}{l} 2 \div 2 = 1 \\ 2 \cdot 2 = 4 \end{array} \quad 2\overline{)2}$$

6. What are these?

   They're _____.

$22 \times 2 = 44$ $5 \times 5 = 25$

8. What are these? $5 \cdot 5 = 25$

   They're _____ problems.

ASK A FRIEND

Please write an addition problem for me.
Please write a subtraction problem for me.
Please write a multiplication problem for me.
Please write a division problem for me.

Science Vocabulary

What words do you know in Science?

I take Science. I am learning new words in Science. They are:

animal bird fish tree plant

_____

In Science we study <u>animals</u>. These are animals.

_____

These are <u>birds</u>.

_____

This is a <u>fish</u>.

_____

These are <u>trees</u>.

_____

These are <u>plants</u>.

_____

Science

What do we study in Science? We study animals. We study birds. We learn about fish. We study trees and plants.

What words do you know in Science?

We study _____*fish*_____ .
animals   fish   birds

What do you study?

We study _____*birds*_____ .

1. We learn about _____ .
   fish   birds   animals

2. We study _____ .
   birds   trees   plants

3. We study _____ .
   plants   animals   trees

4. We learn about _____ .
   animals   birds   fish

5. What do you study?

   We study _____ .

6. What do you study?

   We study _____ .

7. What do you study?

   We study _____ .

8. What do you study?

   We study _____ .

ASK A FRIEND

Please open your Science book.   Please show me a fish.
Please show me a tree.   Please show me a plant.
Please show me a bird.   Please show me an animal.

Here are more new words in Science. They are:

sun star moon telescope microscope

In Science we learn about the <u>sun</u>. This is our sun.

Our sun is a <u>star</u>. We study stars in Science.

We study the <u>moon</u> in Science, too.

We use a <u>telescope</u> in Science. We see the moon through a telescope.

In Science we use a <u>microscope</u>, too.

Science

In Science we study the sun and the moon. We study stars. We see the sun, the moon and other stars through the telescope. In Science we use a microscope, too.

What words do you know in Science?

EXAMPLES:

We study the _____*moon*_____ .
moon   sun   telescope

What is this?

It's a _____*telescope*_____ .

1. We use a _____ .
   telescope   microscope   star

3. We use a _____ .
   microscope   moon   telescope

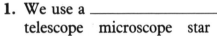

2. We study the _____ .
   moon   sun   telescope

4. We study the _____ .
   stars   moon   microscope

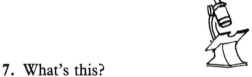

5. What are these?

   They're _____ .

7. What's this?

   It's a _____ .

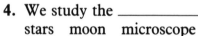

6. What's this?

   It's the _____ .

8. What's this?

   It's the _____ .

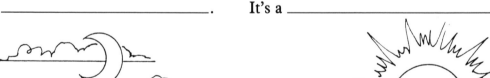

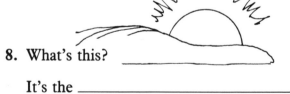

ASK A FRIEND

Please show me how to use a telescope.
Please show me how to use a microscope.

Please show me a picture of our star, the sun.
Please show me a picture of the moon.

20

English Vocabulary

What words do you know in English?

We are learning to speak and listen in English. We talk and listen to learn words in the language. Some of our new words are:

language   speak   word   talk   listen

We are studying English. English is a <u>language</u>.

We want to <u>speak</u> English.

We are learning English <u>words</u>.

We speak English. We <u>talk</u> to our teacher.

We <u>listen</u> to English, too.

English

In this class we are learning the English language. We want to speak English. We are learning English words. In class we speak English. We listen to the teacher. We talk to him, too.

What words do you know in English?

We want to _____*speak*_____ English.
listen   word   speak

1. We _____ to English.
   listen   speak   talk

2. These are English _____.
   listen   speak   words

3. We are studying the English _____.
   speak   language   listen

4. We _____ to our teacher.
   talk   listen   language

5. What do you do in class?

   We _____ English.
   language   listen   speak

6. What are those?

   They are English _____.
   speak   listen   words

7. What do you do?

   We _____ to English.
   talk   listen   words

8. What do you do in class?

   We _____ English.
   speak   language   words

ASK A FRIEND

Please speak English to me.   I want to learn the English language.
I want to listen to English.   Please give me five words in English to learn.

What words do you know in English?

Here are more new words in English:

read   write   sentence   paragraph   composition

We are learning to <u>read</u> English.

We are learning to <u>write</u> English.

We use English words to write <u>sentences</u>.

My name is John.
I am a student.
this is a book.

This is a <u>paragraph</u>.

This is a <u>composition</u>.

Composition

English

We are learning to read and write English. We write English sentences. We write paragraphs with sentences. Our teacher has us write compositions in class.

What words do you know in English?

EXAMPLES:

This is a _____ *paragraph* _____.
sentence   write   paragraph

What are these?

They are _____ *sentences* _____.

My name is John.
I am a student.
I study English.

My name is John.

1. This is a _____.
composition   read   sentence

3. This is a _____.
write   composition   sentence

2. We _____ English.
write   read   sentence

4. We _____ English.
write   read   paragraph

5. What do you do in English?

We _____.

7. What's this?

It's a _____.

6. What's this?

It's a _____.

8. What do you do in English?

We _____.

ASK A FRIEND

Please open your English book and show me a paragraph.
Please read me a sentence.
I want to write the sentence.
Please help me write some sentences.

Computer Vocabulary

What words do you know about the computer?

There are several parts to a computer. Here are some:

keyboard   screen   display   printer   hardware

I talk to the computer on the **keyboard.**

The computer talks to me on the **screen.**

The words on the screen are the **display.**

Sometimes I want the display on paper. Then I use the **printer.**

These parts of the computer are called **hardware.**

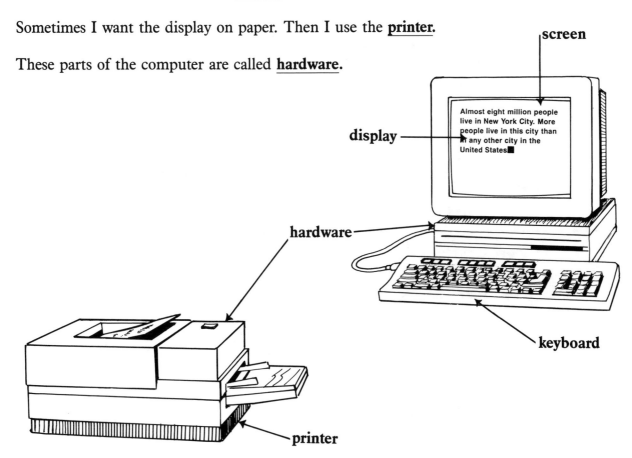

Computer Hardware

In school I use a computer. I talk to the computer on the keyboard. It talks to me with a display on the screen. I copy the words on the screen when I use the printer. These parts of the computer are called hardware.

What words do you know about a computer?

I talk to a ___*computer*___ on the keyboard.
computer   book   friend

What's this?
It's a ___*computer*___.

---

1. The words on the screen are the ___.
   printer   display   screen

2. Parts of the computer are the ___.
   display   paper   hardware

3. When I want the display on paper I use the ___.
   screen   printer   hardware

4. The computer talks to me on the ___.
   printer   keyboard   screen

---

5. What's this?
   It's a ___.

6. What's this?
   It's a ___.

7. What's this?
   It's a ___.

8. What's this?
   It's a ___.

ASK A FRIEND

I want to learn how to use the computer.
Please show me the keyboard.
Please show me the screen.

Please show me the display on the screen.
Where is the printer?
Is this computer hardware?

Computer Vocabulary

Here are more words we use in talking about computers.

boot   disk   disk drive   floppy disk   program   software

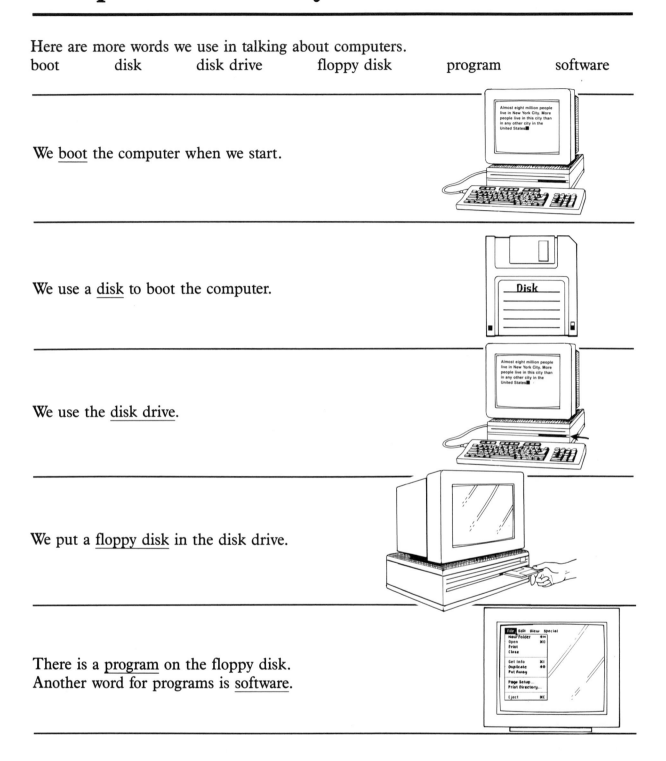

We boot the computer when we start.

We use a disk to boot the computer.

We use the disk drive.

We put a floppy disk in the disk drive.

There is a program on the floppy disk.
Another word for programs is software.

Using Computers

We boot the computer when we start using it. We put a floppy disk in the disk drive. There is a program on the floppy disk. The program is displayed on the screen. Another word for programs is software.

What words do you know about using a computer?

EXAMPLES:

This is a _____ *disk* _____ .
screen   keyboard   disk

What's this?
It's a _____ *program* _____ .

1. We put a disk in the _____ .
   screen   disk drive   boot

2. We _____ the computer to start.
   disk   boot   open

3. There is a _____ on the disk.
   boot   screen   program

4. A program is _____ .
   screen   drive   software

5. What's this?
   It's a _____ .

6. What's software?
   It's a _____ .

7. When we start the computer, what do we do?
   We _____ it.

8. Where do you put the disk?
   We put it in the _____ .

ASK A FRIEND

Please help me use the computer.
Please give me a floppy disk.
I want to boot the computer. Where is the disk drive?
What programs or software do we have?

Art Vocabulary

What words do you know in Art?

We take Art. In Art we use the words:

paint   picture   draw   crayon   color

In Art we learn how to <u>paint</u>. This boy is painting.

We paint <u>pictures</u>. These are pictures.

Sometimes we <u>draw</u>. She is drawing.

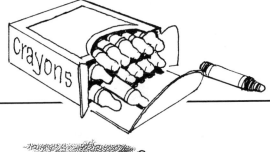

Sometimes we draw with <u>crayons</u>.

There are many <u>colors</u> of crayons.

Art

We have an Art class. In Art we paint pictures or we draw. Sometimes we use crayons in many different colors.

What words do you know in Art?

EXAMPLES:

Crayons are in many _____colors_____ .
crayons   paint   colors

What are these?

They're _____crayons_____ .

1. This is a _____ .
   picture   crayon   color

2. Sometimes we _____ .
   paint   draw   color

3. These are _____ .
   pictures   draw   crayons

4. We _____ pictures.
   crayon   color   paint

5. What do we do?

   We _____ .

6. What do we do?

   We _____ .

7. What are these?

   They're _____ .

8. What are these?

   They're _____ .

ASK A FRIEND

What color do you like?
What picture in the room do you like?
Please draw or paint a picture for me.

Music Vocabulary

What words do you know in Music?

Sometimes we take Music. In Music we use the words:

tape   piano   play   sing   song

In Music sometimes we listen to <u>tapes</u>.

Sometimes we listen to the <u>piano</u>.

Our teacher <u>plays</u> the piano.

Our teacher plays, and we <u>sing</u>.

We sing <u>songs</u>.

Music

    We take Music, too. In Music class we listen to tapes. Sometimes we listen to the piano. Our teacher plays the piano, and we sing. We sing many different songs.

What words do you know in Music?

EXAMPLES:

We sing _____*songs*_____ .
sings   songs   tapes
What do you listen to?
We listen to the _____*piano*_____ .

1. We listen to the _____ .
    piano   tape   sing

3. We listen to _____ .
    pianos   tapes   plays

2. We _____ .
    play   song   sing

4. Our teacher _____ the piano.
    sings   piano   plays

5. What does the teacher do?

The teacher _____ the piano.

7. What do you do?

We _____ .

6. What do you listen to?

We listen to _____ .

8. What do you sing?

We sing _____ .

ASK A FRIEND

Do you play the piano?
Do you like to sing?
What song do you like?
Do you have a tape of that song?

Social Studies—Maps

What words do you know in Social Studies?

In Social Studies we are learning to read maps. We know these map words:

direction   north   south   east   west

A map has directions.

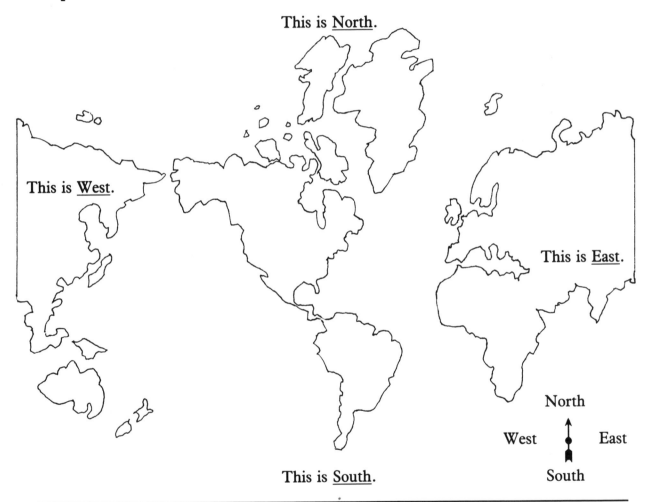

This is <u>North</u>.

This is <u>West</u>.

This is <u>East</u>.

This is <u>South</u>.

North

West   East

South

Social Studies Maps

This is a map of the world. Maps have directions. Every map has a north, a south, an east and a west. We live in North America. There is a South America, too.

What words do you know in Social Studies?

1. Write the directions on this map:

EXAMPLE: This is _____*north*_____.

This is _____.

This is _____.

This is _____.

2. Draw a map of a country you know. Write the directions
on the map.

N _____

W _____   E _____

S _____

ASK A FRIEND

Look at your map.   Where is South?
Where is North?   Where is West?
Where is East?

What words do you know in Social Studies?

Here are more words we use in reading maps in Social Studies:

road   highway   bridge   lake   building

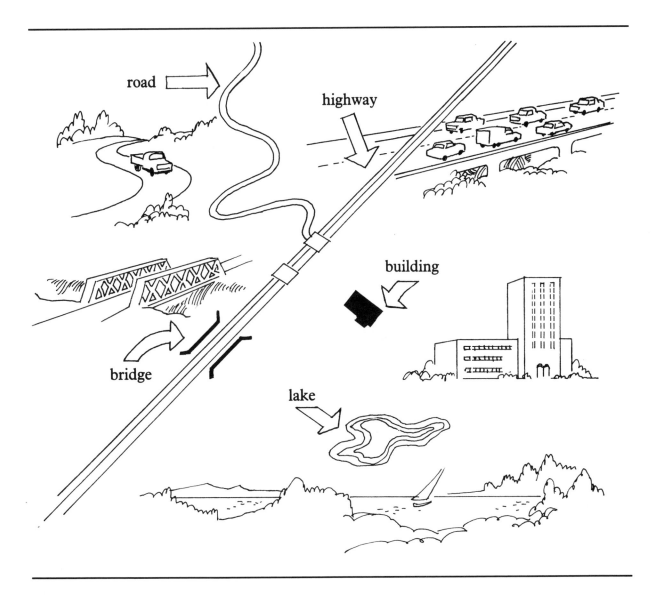

Social Studies Maps

You can see many things on maps. Some maps have the roads and the highways. Some maps have lakes and bridges. Some maps have important buildings, too.

What words do you know in Social Studies?

1. Write the new words on the map:

bridge

EXAMPLE: road

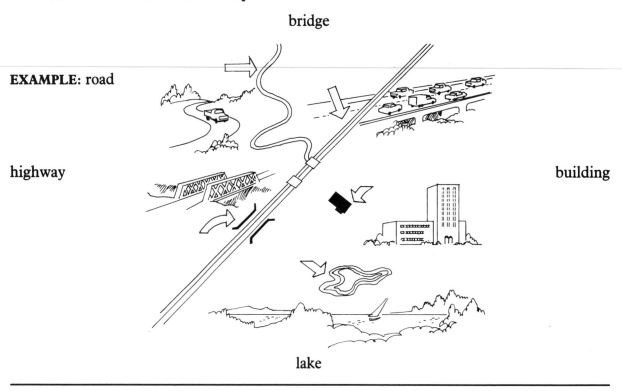

highway

building

lake

2. Draw a map. Draw a line to the word for each part of your map.

road

highway

bridge

lake

building

ASK A FRIEND

Look at your map.   Where is the bridge?
Where is the road?   Where is the lake?
Where is the highway?   Where is the building?

What words do you know in Math?

Here are more words we know in Math:

plus   minus   equal   greater than   less than

$$\begin{array}{r} 65 \\ +\,42 \\ \hline 107 \end{array}$$

In Math we write addition problems with a <u>plus</u>. This is a plus sign.

$341 (+) 802 = 1,143$

+

In Math we write subtraction problems with a <u>minus</u>. This is a minus sign.

$444 (-) 123 = 321$

$$\begin{array}{r} 77 \\ -\,16 \\ \hline 61 \end{array}$$

▭

In some Math problems we write an <u>equal</u>. This is an equal sign.

$22 \times 2 (=) 44$

$5 \times 5 (=) 25$

$5 \cdot 5 (=) 25$

═

In some Math problems we have a <u>greater than</u>. This is a "greater than" sign.

$5 > 3$ $10 > 5$ $7 > 6$

In some Math problems we have a <u>less than</u>. This is a "less than" sign.

$3 < 5$ $5 < 10$ $6 < 7$

Math

We write many different signs in Math. We have a plus sign and a minus sign. We have an equal sign. We have a sign for "greater than" and a sign for "less than," too.

What words do you know in Math?

EXAMPLES:

This is _____an equal_____ sign.
an equal   a minus   a "less than"

What is this sign?

It's _____a "less than"_____ sign.

1. This is _____ sign.
   a minus   an equal   a "less than"

3. This is _____ sign.
   a minus   a plus   a "greater than"

2. This is _____ sign.
   a "less than"   a minus   a plus

4. This is _____ sign.
   a "greater than"   an equal   a plus

5. What's this sign?

   It's _____ sign.

7. What's this sign?

   It's _____ sign.

6. What's this sign?

   It's _____ sign.

8. What's this sign?

   It's _____ sign.

ASK A FRIEND

Please write two numbers.
Which number is greater than the other?
Which number is less than the other?
Please write one number plus another number. What do they equal?
Please write one number minus another number. What do they equal?

Here are more words we use in Math:

total   fraction   whole   decimal   percent

When we add we get a <u>total</u>. This is a total. $341 + 802 = 1,143$ $\begin{array}{r} 65 \\ +42 \\ \hline 107 \end{array}$

Some problems are in <u>fractions</u>. These are fractions. $\frac{1}{2}$ $\frac{1}{3}$ $\frac{1}{4}$ $\frac{1}{5}$

These are numbers. They are <u>whole</u> <u>numbers</u>. They are not fractions. $1, 2, 3, 4, 5, 6, 7, 8, 9, 10$

These are <u>decimals</u>. $.5 \quad .8 \quad .2 \quad .4$

These are <u>percents</u>. They have a percent sign. $5\% \quad 10\% \quad 12\% \quad 25\%$

Math

We are learning how to do more Math problems. When we add we get a total. We add fractions and whole numbers, too. We are learning how to do decimal and percent problems, too.

What words do you know in Math?

EXAMPLES:

This is a ___*decimal*___ .
fraction   percent sign   decimal

What is this?

It's a ___*fraction*___ .

1. This is a _____ .
   percent   total   fraction

3. This is a _____ .
   whole number   fraction   total

2. This is a _____ .
   fraction   decimal   percent sign

4. This is a _____ .
   fraction   decimal   percent sign

5. What's this?

   It's a _____ .

7. What's this?

   It's a _____ .

6. What's this?

   It's a _____ .

8. What's this?

   It's a _____ .

ASK A FRIEND

Please add five and ten. What is the total?
Please add two fractions. What is the total?
Please write a number with a decimal. Change it to a percent.

Science Vocabulary–Earth

What words do you know in Science?

We are learning more words in Science. They are:
flower grow season weather rain

In science we are studying flowers. This is a
<u>flower.</u>

We are learning how a flower <u>grows.</u> This
flower is growing.

We are learning about <u>seasons.</u> There are
growing seasons.

The <u>weather</u> in every season is different.

Sometimes there is sun. Sometimes there is
<u>rain.</u>

sun   rain

Science

We are learning about flowers in Science. Flowers grow
in the growing season. The weather in a growing season is
important. Flowers need sunshine and rain to grow.

What words do you know in Science?

EXAMPLES:

Flowers _____*grow*_____.

season   grow   weather

What does every season have?

Every season has different ___*weather*___.

1. This is _____.
   flower   grow   rain

3. This is a _____.
   rain   flower   season

2. There are different _____.
   flowers   seasons   rains

4. Every season has different _____.
   season   rain   weather

5. What's this?

   It's a _____.

6. What do flowers do?

   They _____.

7. What's this?

   It's _____.

8. When do flowers grow?

   They grow in the growing _____.

ASK A FRIEND

Please open your Science book.
Please show me a flower?
In what season do flowers grow?

What weather is good for flowers?
Do they need rain?

42

Science Vocabulary–Weather

What words do you know in Science?

Here are more new words in Science:
temperature up hot down cold

In Science we are learning about temperature.

Sometimes the temperature goes <u>up</u>.

When the temperature goes up, it is <u>hot</u>.

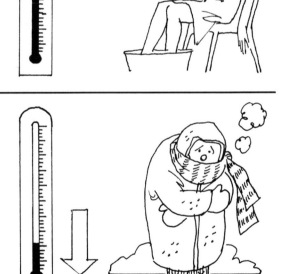

Sometimes the temperature goes <u>down</u>.

When the temperature goes down, it is <u>cold</u>.

Science

The temperature is different in different seasons. In Science we are learning that when the temperature goes up, it is hot. When the temperature goes down, it is cold.

What words do you know in Science?

In Science we are
learning about ___*temperature*___.
up   temperature   down

Is the weather hot or cold?

It's _____*cold*_____.

1. It is _____.
hot   cold   down

3. It is _____.
hot   cold   up

2. The temperature is going _____.
up   hot   down

4. The temperature is going _____.
up   cold   down

5. Is the temperature going up or down?

It's _____.

7. Is the temperature going up or down?

It's _____.

6. Is the weather hot or cold?

It's _____.

8. What do we learn from this?

We learn the _____.

ASK A FRIEND

What happens when the temperature goes up?
What happens when the temperature goes down?
Do you like hot or cold weather?

English Vocabulary–Punctuation

What words do you know in English?

Here are more words we are learning in English:

punctuation period letter capital small

We are learning about <u>punctuation</u> in English.

When we write a sentence we end with a <u>period</u>. This is a period.

I am a student.
You are the teacher.

These are <u>letters</u>. *A* is a letter. *Z* is a letter, too.

A b C D E F g H i j K l
m N o P Q r S t U V w
X y Z

Every sentence begins with a <u>capital</u> letter. *I* is a capital letter. *Y* is a capital letter, too.

I am a student.
You are the teacher.

These are <u>small</u> letters. The letter *a* is a small letter, and *o* is, too.

I am a student.
You are the teacher.

English

We are learning about punctuation in English. We write sentences. They begin with a capital letter. They end with a period.

What words do you know in English?

1. Add the periods in this paragraph.

EXAMPLE:

I am a student I am learning a new language, English

I am a student. I am learning a new language, English.

    My teacher is Ms. James She is teaching me about punctu-
ation I know what a capital letter is I know when to use it,
too I like English

2. Copy the paragraph. Change the letter at the beginning of each sentence to a capital.

EXAMPLE:

i am a student.   i am learning a new language, English.
I am a student.   I am learning a new language, English.

in English we are writing sentences. sentences begin with a capital letter. sentences end
with a period. this is part of punctuation.

_____

_____

_____

_____

_____

ASK A FRIEND

Please open your English book.
Please show me a sentence.
Does the sentence begin with a capital letter?
Does the sentence end with a period?
Please show me a small letter.

What words do you know in English?

Here are more words we use in English:

comma   question mark   date   letter   signature

Here is more punctuation. This is a <u>comma</u>.

This is a <u>question mark</u>.

We use a comma in the <u>date</u>. This is a date.

SEPTEMBER 1994

September 3, 1994

We use the date in a <u>letter</u>. This is a letter.

In a letter, we write our name. This is the <u>signature</u>.

English

In English punctuation we use the period, the comma and the question mark. We use them in writing letters. When we write letters we always write the date and the signature.

What words do you know in English?

EXAMPLE: This is a _____*comma*_____ .
question mark   period   comma

September 3, 1994

Charlie Loo

1. This is a _____ .
comma   date   signature

3. This is a _____ .
date   comma   signature

2. This is a _____ .
question mark   period   comma

4. This is a _____ .
date   letter   signature

Draw a line from the word to the part of the letter.

WORDS

5. comma

6. question mark

7. date

8. signature

February 10, 1993

Dear Jane,

How are you? I'm fine. I want to hear how you are doing. How is your family?

Please write and tell me the news.

Love,

Nancy Martinez

ASK A FRIEND

Please open your English book.
Please show me a comma.
Please show me a question mark.
What is the date today?
Please write your signature for me.

Social Studies—States

What words do you know in Social Studies?

In Social Studies we are learning about the different states.
We know the

Northeastern, Mid-Atlantic and Southern states.

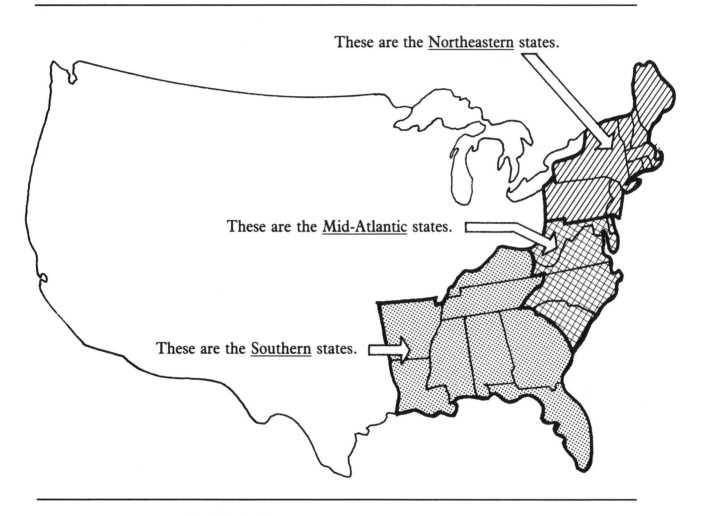

These are the <u>Northeastern</u> states.

These are the <u>Mid-Atlantic</u> states.

These are the <u>Southern</u> states.

Social Studies

In Social Studies we are learning about the regions of the United States. The Northeastern states are Connecticut, Maine, Massachusetts, New Hampshire, New Jersey, New York, Pennsylvania, Rhode Island and Vermont. The Mid-Atlantic states are Delaware, Maryland, North Carolina, South Carolina, Virginia and West Virginia. The Southern states are Alabama, Arkansas, Florida, Georgia, Kentucky, Louisiana, Mississippi and Tennessee.

What words do you know in Social Studies?

1. Draw a line to the states from the word for that region of the country:

Northeastern   Mid-Atlantic   Southern

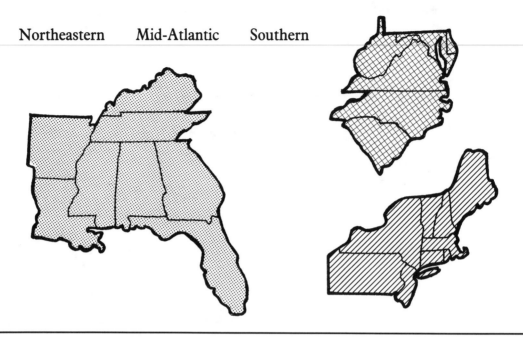

2. Draw a line from the word for a region of the country to the states in that part of the country.

Northeastern	Delaware, Maryland, North Carolina, South Carolina, Virginia, West Virginia
Mid-Atlantic	Connecticut, Maine, Massachusetts, New Hampshire, New Jersey, New York, Pennsylvania, Rhode Island, Vermont
Southern	Alabama, Arkansas, Florida, Georgia, Kentucky, Louisiana, Mississippi, Tennessee

ASK A FRIEND

Please name a Northeastern state.
Please name a Mid-Atlantic state.
Please name a Southern state.
In what region of the country is New York?
In what region of the country is Florida?
In what region of the country is Virginia?

What words do you know in Social Studies?

In Social Studies we are learning about the different states.
We know the

Midwestern, Southwestern and Western states.

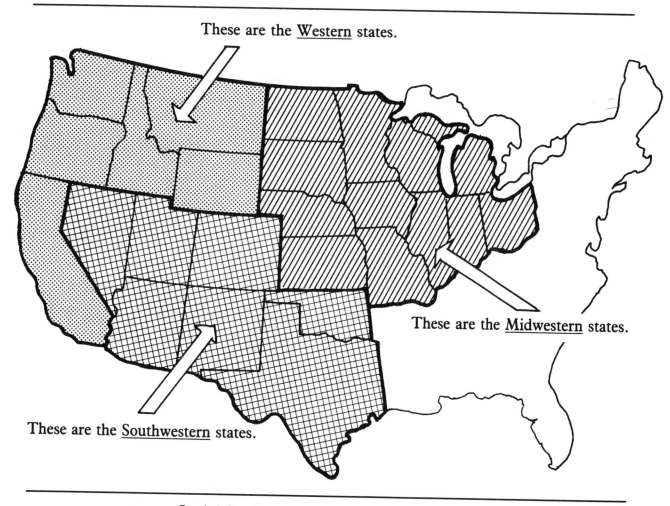

These are the <u>Western</u> states.

These are the <u>Midwestern</u> states.

These are the <u>Southwestern</u> states.

Social Studies

In Social Studies we are learning about the regions of the United States. The Midwestern states are Illinois, Indiana, Iowa, Kansas, Michigan, Minnesota, Missouri, Nebraska, North Dakota, Ohio, South Dakota and Wisconsin. The Southwestern states are Arizona, Colorado, Nevada, New Mexico, Oklahoma, Texas and Utah. The Western states are California, Idaho, Montana, Oregon, Washington and Wyoming. There are two more separate states: Alaska and Hawaii.

What words do you know in Social Studies?

1. Draw a line to the states from the word for that part of the country:

Midwestern   Southwestern   Western

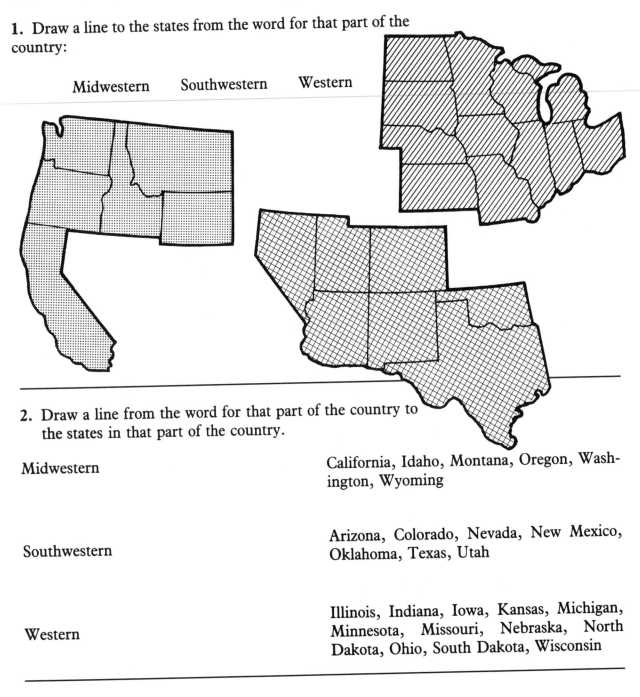

2. Draw a line from the word for that part of the country to the states in that part of the country.

Midwestern

California, Idaho, Montana, Oregon, Washington, Wyoming

Southwestern

Arizona, Colorado, Nevada, New Mexico, Oklahoma, Texas, Utah

Western

Illinois, Indiana, Iowa, Kansas, Michigan, Minnesota, Missouri, Nebraska, North Dakota, Ohio, South Dakota, Wisconsin

ASK A FRIEND

Please name a Midwestern state.
Please name a Southwestern state.
Please name a Western state.
In what region of the country is California?
In what region of the country is Texas?
In what region of the country is Michigan?

Math Word Problems

What do you understand in Math?

In Math some problems are in numbers. Some problems are in words. We are learning to do word problems in addition.

NUMBER PROBLEM: 2 + 3 = 5

WORD PROBLEM: There are 2 boys in the Math class. There are 3 girls in the Math class, too. How many students are there in the Math class?

ANSWER: 2 boys + 3 girls = 5 students

NUMBER PROBLEM: 1 + 1 + 4 = 6

WORD PROBLEM: In my family, there are my mother, my father and four children. How many people are there in my family?

ANSWER: 1 mother + 1 father + 4 children = 6 people

NUMBER PROBLEM: 23 + 18 = 41

WORD PROBLEM: Ms. Jones' class has twenty-three students. There are 18 students in Mr. Andrews' class. How many students are there in the two classes?

ANSWER: 23 students + 18 students = 41 students

In Math problems we can read all these number words:

one	six	eleven	sixteen	thirty	eighty
two	seven	twelve	seventeen	forty	ninety
three	eight	thirteen	eighteen	fifty	(one) hundred
four	nine	fourteen	nineteen	sixty	(one) thousand
five	ten	fifteen	twenty	seventy	zero

What do you understand in Math?

EXAMPLE:

Ali has two books and Cheng has three.
How many books do Ali and Cheng have?

ANSWER: _____ *2 books + 3 books = 5 books* _____

---

1. Cristos has three brothers and four sisters. How many brothers and sisters does he have?

   ANSWER: _____

2. Lucia is walking to school with her friends. There are three boys and four girls. How many friends are there?

   ANSWER: _____

3. The teacher is giving pencils to her students. There are ten boys and twelve girls in the class. How many pencils does the teacher need?

   ANSWER: _____

4. There are six Western states, eleven Midwestern states and six Southwestern states. How many states are there in the West, Midwest and Southwest?

   ANSWER: _____

---

5. Write the word for each number:

0 *Zero*	7 _____	14 _____	30 _____
1 _____	8 _____	15 _____	40 _____
2 _____	9 _____	16 _____	50 _____
3 _____	10 _____	17 _____	
4 _____	11 _____	18 _____	
5 _____	12 _____	19 _____	
6 _____	13 _____	20 _____	

ASK A FRIEND

How many are fifty-one and seventy-eight?
How many are thirteen and thirty?
How many are fifty and fifteen?

How many are six and seventeen?
How many are twenty and seventy?
How many are eighteen and eighty?

In Math we are learning to do word problems in subtraction.

NUMBER PROBLEM:	25 − 10 = 15
WORD PROBLEM:	There are twenty-five students in our class. There are ten boys. How many girls are there?
ANSWER:	25 − 10 = 15

NUMBER PROBLEM:	8 − 4 = 4
WORD PROBLEM:	The Sanchez family has eight children. There are four brothers. How many sisters are there?
ANSWER:	8 − 4 = 4

NUMBER PROBLEM:	20 − 10 = 10
WORD PROBLEM:	There are twenty rooms in our school. Ten rooms are on the second floor. How many rooms are there on the first floor?
ANSWER:	20 − 10 = 10

We can read these number words in our Math problems:

first	fourth	seventh	tenth
second	fifth	eighth	(one) millionth
third	sixth	ninth	(one) billionth

What do you understand in Math?

There are seven days in the week. We don't go to school on
two days. How many days do we go to school?

ANSWER: _____ *7 days − 2 days = 5 days* _____

---

1. Susana has six subjects. She takes three
    before lunch. How many subjects does
    she take after lunch?

    ANSWER: _____

2. There are thirty-five teachers in my
    school. Six of them teach me. How many
    other teachers are there?

    ANSWER: _____

3. Nick has five schoolbooks. One is his
    English book. How many other books
    does he have?

    ANSWER: _____

4. Every week Helmut learns twenty new
    English words. This week he knows ten.
    How many more does he need to learn
    this week?

    ANSWER: _____

---

5. Write the word for each number:

    60 _*sixty*_____

    70 _____

    80 _____

    90 _____

    100 _____

    1,000 _____

    1,000,000 _____

    1,000,000,000 _____

ASK A FRIEND

What is the first letter of the English alphabet?
What grade are you in?
What do you have second period?
Do you eat sixth period?
Who is your third-period teacher?

More Math Word Problems

What do you understand in Math?

We are learning to do word problems in multiplication.

NUMBER PROBLEM: $10 \times 2 = 20$

WORD PROBLEM: There are ten desks in the classroom. Two students sit at each desk. How many students can sit in the classroom?

ANSWER: 10 desks $\times$ 2 students $=$ 20 students

NUMBER PROBLEM: $5 \times 6 = 30$

WORD PROBLEM: The students go to school five days a week. Every day they are in class six hours. How many hours are the students in class every week?

ANSWER: 5 days $\times$ 6 hours a day $=$ 30 hours a week

NUMBER PROBLEM: $5 \times 30 = 150$

WORD PROBLEM: There are five classrooms on the first floor. There are thirty students in every classroom. How many students are there on the first floor?

ANSWER: 5 classrooms $\times$ 30 students $=$ 150 students

The Multiplication Tables

$1 \times 1 = 1$	$2 \times 1 = 2$	$3 \times 1 = 3$	$4 \times 1 = 4$	$5 \times 1 = 5$
$1 \times 2 = 2$	$2 \times 2 = 4$	$3 \times 2 = 6$	$4 \times 2 = 8$	$5 \times 2 = 10$
$1 \times 3 = 3$	$2 \times 3 = 6$	$3 \times 3 = 9$	$4 \times 3 = 12$	$5 \times 3 = 15$
$1 \times 4 = 4$	$2 \times 4 = 8$	$3 \times 4 = 12$	$4 \times 4 = 16$	$5 \times 4 = 20$
$1 \times 5 = 5$	$2 \times 5 = 10$	$3 \times 5 = 15$	$4 \times 5 = 20$	$5 \times 5 = 25$
$1 \times 6 = 6$	$2 \times 6 = 12$	$3 \times 6 = 18$	$4 \times 6 = 24$	$5 \times 6 = 30$
$1 \times 7 = 7$	$2 \times 7 = 14$	$3 \times 7 = 21$	$4 \times 7 = 28$	$5 \times 7 = 35$
$1 \times 8 = 8$	$2 \times 8 = 16$	$3 \times 8 = 24$	$4 \times 8 = 32$	$5 \times 8 = 40$
$1 \times 9 = 9$	$2 \times 9 = 18$	$3 \times 9 = 27$	$4 \times 9 = 36$	$5 \times 9 = 45$
$1 \times 10 = 10$	$2 \times 10 = 20$	$3 \times 10 = 30$	$4 \times 10 = 40$	$5 \times 10 = 50$
$1 \times 11 = 11$	$2 \times 11 = 22$	$3 \times 11 = 33$	$4 \times 11 = 44$	$5 \times 11 = 55$
$1 \times 12 = 12$	$2 \times 12 = 24$	$3 \times 12 = 36$	$4 \times 12 = 48$	$5 \times 12 = 60$

What do you understand in Math?

EXAMPLE:

Every student in the class has three books. There are 10 students in the class. How many books are there?

ANSWER: *3 books × 10 students = 30 books*

1. In the cafeteria every student eats two sandwiches. There are thirty students. How many sandwiches do they need?

   ANSWER: _____

2. Every student in English is writing two letters. There are eight students. How many letters are there?

   ANSWER: _____

3. The Art teacher is giving three crayons to every student. There are twelve students in the class. How many crayons does the class need?

   ANSWER: _____

4. Our school has five rooms on every floor. There are four floors. How many rooms are there?

   ANSWER: _____

5. Finish the multiplication tables for 1, 2, 3, 4 and 5. Say each problem.

   $1 \times 1 = 1$ $2 \times 1 = 2$ $3 \times 1 = 3$ $4 \times 1 = 4$ $5 \times 1 = 5$

   _____

   _____

   _____

   _____

   _____

ASK A FRIEND

Please multiply five and six. What is the answer?
Please multiply two and ten. What is the answer?
Please multiply four and eight. What is the answer?
Please multiply three and seven. What is the answer?
Please multiply one and twelve. What is the answer?

In Math we are learning to do word problems in division.

NUMBER PROBLEM: 20 ÷ 2 = 10

WORD PROBLEM: There are twenty students in the class. Two students sit at every desk. How many desks are there?

ANSWER: 20 students ÷ 2 students at desk = 10 desks

NUMBER PROBLEM: 30 ÷ 6 = 5

WORD PROBLEM: There are thirty students eating in the cafeteria. The cafeteria has six tables. The same number of students sits at each one. How many students are sitting at every table?

ANSWER: 30 students ÷ 6 tables = 5 students at every table

NUMBER PROBLEM: 30 ÷ 5 = 6

WORD PROBLEM: Simon walks five blocks to school every morning. Each block has the same number of buildings. There are thirty buildings on his way. How many buildings are in every block?

ANSWER: 30 buildings ÷ 5 blocks = 6 buildings in every block

The Multiplication Tables

6 × 1 = 6	7 × 1 = 7	8 × 1 = 8	9 × 1 = 9	10 × 1 = 10
6 × 2 = 12	7 × 2 = 14	8 × 2 = 16	9 × 2 = 18	10 × 2 = 20
6 × 3 = 18	7 × 3 = 21	8 × 3 = 24	9 × 3 = 27	10 × 3 = 30
6 × 4 = 24	7 × 4 = 28	8 × 4 = 32	9 × 4 = 36	10 × 4 = 40
6 × 5 = 30	7 × 5 = 35	8 × 5 = 40	9 × 5 = 45	10 × 5 = 50
6 × 6 = 36	7 × 6 = 42	8 × 6 = 48	9 × 6 = 54	10 × 6 = 60
6 × 7 = 42	7 × 7 = 49	8 × 7 = 56	9 × 7 = 63	10 × 7 = 70
6 × 8 = 48	7 × 8 = 56	8 × 8 = 64	9 × 8 = 72	10 × 8 = 80
6 × 9 = 54	7 × 9 = 63	8 × 9 = 72	9 × 9 = 81	10 × 9 = 90
6 × 10 = 60	7 × 10 = 70	8 × 10 = 80	9 × 10 = 90	10 × 10 = 100
6 × 11 = 66	7 × 11 = 77	8 × 11 = 88	9 × 11 = 99	10 × 11 = 110
6 × 12 = 72	7 × 12 = 84	8 × 12 = 96	9 × 12 = 108	10 × 12 = 120

What do you understand in Math?

EXAMPLE:

Mr. Finney has eighty students. He teaches four classes all the same size. How many students are in each class?

ANSWER: _80 students ÷ 4 classes = 20 students in each class_

---

1. There are twenty rooms in the school. There are five rooms on each floor. How many floors are in the school building?

    ANSWER: _____

2. There are six machines in the shop and eighteen students. How many students should work at each machine?

    ANSWER: _____

3. Jacques has fifteen pages to read in his Social Studies book. He has three days to do the work. How many pages a day should he read?

    ANSWER: _____

4. There are ten pieces of fish for dinner and five people at the table. How many pieces can each person eat?

    ANSWER: _____

---

5. Finish the multiplication tables for 6, 7, 8, 9 and 10. Say each problem.

$6 \times 1 = 6$ $\qquad$ $7 \times 1 = 7$ $\qquad$ $8 \times 1 = 8$ $\qquad$ $9 \times 1 = 9$ $\qquad$ $10 \times 1 = 10$

_____

_____

_____

_____

_____

ASK A FRIEND

Please divide fifty-four by nine. What is the answer?
Please divide one hundred twenty by ten. What is the answer?
Please divide sixty-three by seven. What is the answer?
Please divide fifty-four by nine. What is the answer?
Please divide thirty-six by six. What is the answer?
